FIRST FLUSH
SAMPLE INSPIRATIONAL POETRY

SELECTED INSPIRATIONAL POEMS
BOOK ONE

ORNA ROSS

Copyright © 2019 Orna Ross
The authors's moral rights have been asserted.
All rights reserved.

Font Publications is the publishing imprint for Orna Ross's fiction and poetry, the Go Creative! books and planners and Alliance of Independent Authors publishing guides.

All Enquiries: sarah@ornaross.com

FIRST FLUSH
SAMPLE INSPIRATIONAL POETRY
E-book: 978-1-913349-65-3
Paperback: 978-1-913349-66-0
Large Print: 978-1-913349-67-7
Hardback: 978-1-913349-68-4
Audiobook: 978-1-913349-69-1

CONTENTS

Selected Inspirational Poetry	1
QUESTIONS	
Where are you?	5
Love Hurts?	7
LABORS	
Whatever	11
Writer At Work	13
Followings	15
HISTORIES	
A Standing Stone In Gladstone Park	19
Halo	23
HAIKU MOMENTS	
About my haiku	27
haiku i	29
haiku ii	31
haiku iii	33
GIFTS & BLESSINGS	
First Flush	37
Underscore	39
Turning Point	41
Let's Keep in Touch	43
Award Winning Inspirational Poetry	45
Acknowledgments	49
About The Poet	51

SELECTED INSPIRATIONAL POETRY

READING INSPIRATIONAL POETRY

Poetry. We need it more than ever these days, as media and internet threaten to engulf us in words designed to dupe, and distract, and induce. We can choose to take in instead words crafted by poets, with the very opposite kinds of intention.

That's my choice.

For a long time now, I've limited my intake of what the world calls "news", and prefer to scroll my Instagram or Tumblr stream instead, which is full of the work of today's poets. Or to curl up with a collection of words written decades, centuries or even millennia ago. And to add a few of my own crafted words to the flow.

Day by day, I choose words intended to console, inspire, illuminate and enlighten. The lyrical, magical, mystical medium we call poetry.

INSPIRATIONAL POETRY

I read and write all kinds of poems but I love most the genre called inspirational, poems that are not religious but spiritual, written to inspire. I don't believe in gods made in human image. I believe only in what I've experienced myself as real: the spirit that created me creating through me.

Inspiration is the child of spirit and by definition, it is beyond definition. It can't be captured, just experienced. And it is experienced not by effort, but by grace.

That's where poems come in. The aim is not to pin anything down but to point up the space between the words. That's where the inspiration happens. And that's my creative intention as I write.

It's in this spirit that I offer you this short, free chapbook with its samples of the many kinds of poems I write: questions, labors, histories, haiku moments, gifts and blessings.

My hope is that it will add a little truth, magic or mystery to your day. That it will not only divert you but also sustain you. That you will read them aloud, copy lines into your f-r-e-e-writing notebook or journal, pass them onto your friends. This, to me, is the highest praise, dearer than any prestigious awards or literary criticism.

I hope too that this book will encourage you to read more motivational and inspirational poetry.

And to reread. Poems have a protean life, they change with us.

Until next time, may your life be filled with poetry!

PS: If you like the poems in this book, do consider becoming a poetry patron at OrnaRoss.com/poetry-patrons so you can receive an exclusive poetry chapbook, just for you, and other books and bonuses each month.

QUESTIONS

WHERE ARE YOU?

Where are you? The splendor of creation
awaits. Beauty veiled, she dallies, playing
with the wings of birds passing, swaying
her hips with the wind, wanting to dance,
to bring you music from planets and clouds.

Call her by right name, hear her answer.
Male or female, she is yours: lingering,
singing and playing, holding out
a braceleted hand, all tinkle and glint.

She wants to roll ecstasy over and under
your skin, swirl bubblings into your blood,
breathe you away through the waves of the ages.

You can stay where you are (where are you?)
and just listen. No, don't even listen, just be.
Unmask. That is all. She will offer herself,

unasked and unasking. No demands
from her, ever, to know: where are you?

LOVE HURTS?

Love hurts, they say.
I say, no way.
The only thing that never hurts
is love.

Lust festers,
envy bites.
Loss skewers,
rejection spikes.
Passion burns,
craving seethes.
Romance dazzles,
lonesome bleeds.
Well yes, indeed.
But none of the above
is love.

Love helps,
love lights.
Love warms,

love rights.
Love soothes,
love feeds.
Love calms,
love heals.

Yes,
what will heal
the sting of pain,
and make your life
feel good again,
again, again,
and oh yes, yet again,
is love.

Love hurts, they say.
I say no way.
The only thing that never hurts
is love.

LABORS

WHATEVER

Whatever you do,
my dear maker,
don't go looking for yourself,
or seeking to improve.
You are not to be found,
and nothing whatever in you
needs to be fixed.

You, my beauty, are
what you are
and whatever you are
currently
creating from that.

Don't allow yourself
to be riven.

You don't need
to be political,
or intellectual.

Charitable
or emblematical.
You have no need to repent.
And no reason to revert.
The motion you seek
is one of release.

Relent. Say, in your own way
whatever it was
your ancestors meant
when they declared
god to be good.

And whatever you make
from the undulating being
you've been given,
make it loud. Do it proud.

WRITER AT WORK

I sit into
the open space,
and wait, until
some true words rise,
arrive to take their place
upon the page.
Then off we go.

I curtsey to them
turn them round
then up, then down
as new thoughts show.

Then comes the time
to let them lie,
put them aside.

In later space
to read them cold
to weigh

and measure
and behold.
To oust some out,
bring in some new
and turn them round
and up and down again.

Repeat to need until
they come together,
click to fit each other.
Then meaning swoops,
through layers bound
in sense and sound,
to wrap me round
and tell me what
I never knew
I know.

FOLLOWINGS

Creatives grope through the dark
drawn by the promise of dawn
our way lit by the stars
who smile on our stumbles
know why we seek
and love what our searching creates.

HISTORIES

A STANDING STONE IN GLADSTONE PARK

Longer than forever ago lived
a people whom we, squinting
back through thickets of time,
like to call The Celts. It's said
they worshipped trees,
as ancient people widely did,
as any soulful person must.

And where I come from,
(an island off an island off
the continental shelf of Europe,
a little place a long time
on the outer edge of things)
some of the Celtic ways,
if that is what they were, lasted,
through centuries of stones
and spears, monks
and mothers, mansions,
cottages and bombs, dark
ages and enlightenments, all

the way to our own time.

So I grew up with Cold War
and central heating, nuclear
threat and hippie love, yet still
knowing holy wells, fairy forts, banshees,
Lughnasa and *Bealtaine,*
the real meaning of Halloween.

And then, this morning, on my park run
through my city park, where I live now,
(a metropolis a long time at the heart of things)
I saw a circle of trees, planted in what they say
was the Celtic way to make a sacred grove,
and marked by what is, unmistakably,
a miniature standing stone.

I stepped into the circle, circled
the upright stone, and, full of wonder,
wondered: Who made this?
Which park worker by stealth, or
council boss by stroke of pen,
decreed that it would be?

Well, here it is.
The trees are thriving and
the stone attracts scratchers
with sharp instruments
to pen magic eyes
and declarations of everlasting love.
I've come back to stand beside it now,
an hour from sunset, to lean against it
into the glow of a day not quite over.

And as I do, I know the stone
and all it stands for. Like its big siblings

Stonehenge. Newgrange, the pyramids,
it will outlast us, outlast probably
the knowledge of us.

As the sun sets in Gladstone Park,
this silent outcrop of an ancient way
of worship holds the rush of a great city
and the hush of all the ages,
a monument to that
which is always
moving, never ceasing—
and ever standing, still.

HALO

My brother, Conor, used them
as they should be used, the rings.
Hoops of grey rubber to throw
at numbered hooks on a board
and make the grownups who came
to our place for their daily drink
call out. *Well done!*

To me they were things to twirl
atop my four-year-old
pointing finger, till they flew.
Or to array my arms,
making of me a Sheba, or a Cleopatra.
A princess of places with names
like Abyssinia, or Timbucktoo.
Their open circle of air
was pregnant with everything.

And the black board where
you were supposed to score

the tally was where, up on a barstool,
I liked to chalk my writing.
A. And B. And C.
And where, one day, I was caught
by the moment I now know
will hold me forever rapt:
when meaning came swimming towards me,
in white, shimmering out of black.

Apple!
And Ball!
And Cat!

Behind me, Conor was throwing a ring
and men were calling. *Yes! Score!*
Good man yourself!
while I cast off, sailing away
in language, braceletted wrists aloft.

HAIKU MOMENTS

ABOUT MY HAIKU

Haiku is a popular poetic form that originated in Japan. It's a subtle form, used to capture a moment, often in #nature, through three short lines of present-moment awareness. A poetic snapshot that may draw on sound, touch, taste and smell as well as sight.

A minute of mindfulness, expressed in words.

In #haiku form, the lines of the poem are arranged in a fixed number of syllables. #575 is a common variant; I prefer #373 and that's the form used for the poems here.

Most days I write a haiku or two as a way of generating creative presence (See my book *How to Write Haiku* for more on this). I then post them on my Instagram page using the hashtag: #creativemoments.

Join me there (Instagram.com/ornaross) and share your own #creativemoments in #haiku?

HAIKU I

above a dry
riverbed trees whisper the
sound of water

HAIKU II

evening
dark submerging the dimming
light of day

HAIKU III

lake water
bird in stillness standing
not waiting

GIFTS & BLESSINGS

FIRST FLUSH

Not yet one day old and as we,
with your mother, stare, aching,
at the soft throb of your vulnerable
skull, your neck so soft, too slight, as yet,
to hold your head
but already elegant,
like hers;
as we gaze
at your gossamer brows,
your crystalline skin,
with wonder last felt thirty years before,
at your tiny nails, each one of ten
a pin-point of pure perfection
on your cupped feet and fingers
the sun comes out,
emerging from clouds
we'd failed to notice until then.
Through the window
sunlight passes

for the first time,
across your face,
and with you
we are each illuminated,
all newborn.

UNDERSCORE

This bright early morning
I've come down to the ocean
to let thoughts come undone
in the waves' whoosh and turn.

A long-haired musician
crossed-legged on a stone
smiles up from his guitar
while continuing to strum.

Above us, on the prom
the runners are running
the early road traffic
is starting its hum.

Down here on the strand
with the tide pressing in
young man and his music,
and me: we sit on.

Two faces upturned
to the warmth of the sun
and the sound of the sea
underscoring his song.

TURNING POINT

For Kathy

    May you know many a moment when
    the wind facing strongly into you
    turns
    to brace your back and lift your legs,
    now bearing you along.

    May you know many a moment when
    the sun hidden behind hill and cloud
    breaks
    to let its rays light up your face,
    now turning you warm.

    May you know many a moment when
    the road rising steep and stoney
    crests
    to a grass path turned towards your feet,
    now urging you on.

May you know many a moment when
the rains falling hard on your forehead
lift
to fall soft and light on your heart,
now settling you down

here, where you may know many a moment
of comfort, holding the wind and the sun,
the road and the rain, and holding too
the knowing that each and all
were always turning you towards here
now, always taking you home.

LET'S KEEP IN TOUCH

Enjoyed the poems? Would you like more? If you're online, we have lots of ways to continue the poetic conversation.

UPDATES & BONUSES

I write a new poem every few days and love sharing inspirations and ideas with my poetry pen-friends. My monthly email will bring you my inspirational poetry news and ideas, discounted books, and other pen-friend presents. Follow the link below to become my poetry pen-friend and get a **free e-book**:

OrnaRoss.com/Free-Poetry

PLEASE REVIEW THIS BOOK ONLINE

If you enjoyed this book, please give it a quick review online by visiting the link below and selecting the "Reviews" tab. Your review doesn't have to be long or detailed. A quick star rating and a sentence or two that helps others to understand the value of this book is all that's needed. I appreciate the support more than you know. *Go raibh maith agat!*

OrnaRoss.com/FirstFlush

BECOME A PATRON

I reserve exclusive poems, special offers, and priority access for my patrons on Patreon. If you want monthly poetry chapbooks you can't get anywhere else, plus other books and bonuses, join me on Patreon as a poetry patron. Click the following link for more info on Patreon bonuses:

OrnaRoss.com/Poetry-Patrons

AWARD WINNING INSPIRATIONAL POETRY

Orna Ross: Inspirational Poetry Books

If you like uplifting cadences and brushes with the infinite, treat yourself to more powerful poetry from this award-winning Irish poet.

FROM THE INSPIRATIONAL POETRY SERIES

Keepers

A book of motivational poetry that encourages you to do what you love, spurs you to greatness, picks you up when you fail and lets you know that, yes, you can make it.

"Ross's verse is technically brilliant, emotionally beguiling and, at times, startling." (Kaleem Raja, The View from Here)

To get *Keepers*, visit:

OrnaRoss.com/Keepers

Allowing Now

Covering themes like mindfulness, meditation, and self-compassion, *Allowing Now* explores the perceptions of a poet for whom everyday moments are both a treasure and an opportunity for growth.

"Not just a collection of good poetry… [but]… an exercise in wellness" (Amazon Review)

To get *Allowing Now*, visit:

OrnaRoss.com/AllowingNow

FROM THE 12 POEMS TO INSPIRE SERIES

Bright Star

An illustrated book of poems about births and beginnings. A beautiful gift for Christmas, or for anyone starting anew.

"A lovely, emotional collection, something to treasure." (*The Bookwormery*)

To get *Bright Star*, visit:

OrnaRoss.com/BrightStar

Night Light As It Rises

This illustrated, inspirational gift book explores grief, consolation, and carrying on. A thoughtful gift for hard times.

"Since my mum died I make sure to take time for honouring her and this spoke to that feeling…" (*Cozy Chapters*)

To get *Night Light as It Rises*, visit:
OrnaRoss.com/NightlightAsItRises

Circle of Life

An illustrated gift book of inspirational poems about mothering–a gift for Mother's Day, or anytime, for anyone who gives care.

To get *Circle of Life*, visit:
OrnaRoss.com/CircleOfLife

ACKNOWLEDGMENTS

My thanks to Andrew Brown of Design for Writers for fabulous cover art and design. To the #IndiePoetryPlease community on Instagram, thank you for reading, thank you for writing. To the publishing team: Sarah Begley, Kayleigh Brindley and Dan Parsons, who get the words from me to the readers. To Philip Lynch, first reader and sometime muse. And a special thanks to my patrons on Patreon, who keep the poems coming. With a bow, thank you all. *Sonas libh go léir.*

x Orna

ABOUT THE POET

Orna Ross is an award-winning and bestselling novelist and poet. She writes historical fiction and inspirational poetry and is a founder-director of the Alliance of Independent Authors (ALLi). Born and raised in Wexford, in the south-east corner of Ireland, she now lives and works in London and St Leonard's-on-Sea, in the south-east corner of England.

Find out more at
OrnaRoss.com

amazon.com/author/OrnaRoss
goodreads.com/ornaross
patreon.com/OrnaRoss

www.ingramcontent.com/pod-product-compliance
Lightning Source LLC
Chambersburg PA
CBHW021133080526
44587CB00012B/1271